HOW TO LOOK AFTER YOUR

BUDGIE

A PRACTICAL GUIDE TO CARING FOR YOUR PET, IN STEP-BY-STEP PHOTOGRAPHS

DAVID ALDERTON

ARMADILLO

Introduction

Budgies make great pets. Young budgies are very friendly birds, and it is not difficult to teach them to sit on your finger or even on your shoulder. Better still, unlike other pets such as dogs and cats, budgies can learn to talk and whistle. This can really cheer you up if you've had a bad day! If you decide to have a budgie, you will need to spend time every day feeding your pet, and must clean out the cage at least twice every week. You should also talk and play with your budgie, so that you become good friends, otherwise your pet is likely to be shy, and will not sit on your hand.

Once your budgie has become comfortable in its new surroundings and made friends with you, it may be tame enough to sit on your finger.

Budgies will happily live together as long as they have enough room.

One or two?

Having two budgies means that they will keep each other company. It is better to obtain them at the same time, so they grow up together, because otherwise the new budgie may be bullied by your older pet. Remember also that you will need a larger cage for two budgies, and that they will probably not talk as well as one kept on its own, because they will chatter to each other rather than learning words. You can still tame them easily though, so that eventually both of them may sit on your hand together.

Ideal pets

It will not take very long to look after your budgie every day, and you can keep a budgie even if your home is in the middle of a city. Although budgies sing and talk, their calls are not loud and so will not upset people living close to you. They are also not expensive pets to keep, nor is it usually difficult to find a friend who will look after your budgie if you go away. Most budgies live for six or seven years, although occasionally, they have lived for more than 20 years!

Budgies are small birds and do not need a very large cage. This makes them perfect for keeping indoors, because they do not take up much space.

Budgies eat a mixture of seeds. You will need to replace your bird's food and water every day.

Concerns with cats

It can be harder to have a budgie if you have a cat, because cats naturally hunt birds. However, it is not impossible to keep both animals. You will always need to be sure that your cat is out of the room and the door is closed before you open your budgie's cage. The same thing applies with dogs, although dogs are less likely to try to catch your budgie.

It is important to keep your budgie safe from pet cats.

What is a budgie?

Budgie is short for budgerigar. Budgerigars belong to the parrot family. They have long tail feathers and are sometimes described as parakeets, because true parrots have short, square tails. Budgies originally came from Australia. In the wild they live in large groups called flocks. They often have to fly long distances to find food and water, because the weather in Australia is very hot, and in some areas it might not rain for months or even years.

Wild budgies perch in trees. Their green feathers help them hide among the leaves.

Spotting a budgie

In the wild, budgies have green feathers. Pet budgies have been bred to be a wide range of different shades, but they are still unmistakable. While we like budgies to have bright feathers, their normal green coloration helps them to remain hidden in among the green leaves of trees in the wild. The wavy pattern on their wings makes them look blurry when flying, so that it is harder for birds of prey to see them.

The budgie's eyes may be black or red, depending on the colour variety.

Budgies have dark cheek spots. These form what is known as the "mask".

Budgies have two toes that grip the front of the perch and two that support their weight behind.

Feathers help to keep budgies warm. They are sometimes described as the plumage.

The long flight feathers at the bottom of the wings help budgies to fly well.

How budgies got their name

The native Aboriginal people of Australia used to hunt budgies. They called these parakeets *betcherygah*. This Aboriginal word actually means "good food"!

This is a special temporary cage used for show budgies. It is designed so that the judges can see the birds easily.

Show birds

Some breeders who want to breed particular types house their pairs in special breeding cages, rather than allowing them to choose their own mates. Budgie owners who enter their birds into competitions also breed birds in this way. Some even have a special bird room, where they keep all their cages and train their birds for shows.

Around the world

Budgies were brought from Australia to Europe on a ship over 150 years ago. Europeans who had made the long journey to Australia knew these little parakeets could talk well, and before long, they were very popular as pets. Budgies did well living in captivity and were easy to keep. They were happy to breed in large enclosures called aviaries. They are now the most popular pet bird in the world.

Sky blue budgies are now very popular, although budgies of any coloration can be taught to talk and whistle well.

Boy or girl?

You can tell the difference between male and female budgies very easily. Adult males, called cocks, have blue or sometimes purple ceres. The cere is the fleshy area above the bill. If you look closely here, you will see two tiny holes, which are the budgie's nostrils. Female budgies, or hens, have brownish ceres, which turn darker when they are laying eggs.

Adult male and female budgies have different ceres. The bird on the left is a female. The one on the right is a male.

Budgie varieties

One of the reasons why budgies are such popular pets is that they can now be bred in many thousands of colorations and patterns. There are even crested budgies as well, although these are quite scarce. The first plumage changes were seen in flocks of wild budgies, but in the wild, budgies that stand out because they look brighter are likely to be caught by predators.

This budgie is a pied yellowface grey. Pied describes the patch of yellow over the grey body.

Blue or green

Budgies can be many different shades. They are usually green with yellow faces, or blue with white faces. However, these basic shades come in different gradations. Green birds can be light green, dark green, olive, or dull green. Blue birds can be sky blue, cobalt, mauve or violet, or can even be closer to grey. Some blue birds have yellow, instead of white faces. One of the most attractive of all the colour combinations is the yellow-faced violet bird.

How new varieties are created

In the wild, budgies are green, but sometimes chicks with unusual plumages appear in their nests. In the 1870s, breeders started to mate these unusual budgies with each other to create more just like them. Even today, new plumage varieties still appear occasionally, and cause a lot of excitement, partly because they are quite unexpected. One of the latest, which is still very rare, has a body that resembles coal!

This pretty variety of budgie is called an opaline spangle sky blue.

The yellowface cobalt variety is a darker shade than the sky blue budgies.

Other shades

Some budgies have no pigment in their bodies. This means that they are pure white, with pink legs and feet and red eyes, too. They are called albinos. Pure yellow budgies with red eyes, known as lutinos, are also very popular. Pied budgies have white or yellow patches breaking up their blue or green coloration. If you choose a pied as a pet, you can be sure that there will not be another budgie anywhere with exactly the same patterning!

Albino budgies are completely white. Their skin is pink because of the blood under it.

Crested budgies

There are three different types of crested budgie. The tufted variety has a raised tuft of feathers on its head. The most popular variety is the full circular crested, which has raised feathers that hang down in the shape of a circle on the top of its head. In the case of the half circular variety, the crest forms just half a circle here.

This circular crested light green budgie is one of the few varieties that has a crest of feathers on its head.

This whitewing violet has a very pale pattern on its wings and back. The dark patterns on wild budgies help them blend into their background and hide from danger.

Markings

The feathers on budgies' wings are usually black with yellow or white edges, and on the backs of their heads they have black stripes called bars. However, breeders have produced new varieties with different patterns. The markings can be much paler than usual, as in the case of yellow-wing greens and whitewing blues, or they can be brown, as in the case of cinnamon budgies. Spangle varieties have a different pattern of black on their feathers, giving a mottled effect.

Choosing your budgie

It is very important not to rush into choosing a budgie, otherwise you could end up being disappointed. The important thing to remember is that you must start off with a young bird, between six and nine weeks old. Older birds will not be as easy to tame, nor are they likely to prove to be such talented talkers. The time of year can be important also, because although budgies may nest at any stage, the largest choice of chicks will be available during the summer months, when most pairs breed.

You may have to wait a while to get a young budgie with an unusual plumage. Green budgies are more common.

You should check that the bird you are going to buy is alert and chirpy and is in good health.

Bright eyes, with no signs of swelling

Upper bill extends over lower bill, rather than tucking inside it

Plumage in good condition

Perching without any discomfort

Nails on each toe

Where to go

Many pet stores sell budgies, as do bird farms, where there may be a wider range offered. Alternatively, you may be able to find a breeder in your area. Breeders often advertise in a local newspaper, or you could contact a bird club in your local area to ask if any of their members breed this type of parakeet.

When you are buying a bird, it is a good idea to take someone along with you who knows about them and can give you advice. Make sure you know what to look out for, so you can choose a budgie that is healthy and which has not been with other birds that may be ill.

Recognizing a chick

Young budgies do not look like their parents. The wavy lines on the head extend right down to the cere at this age. This is why young budgies are often called barheads. There may also be a brownish tip to the bill, especially in blue and grey budgies. When there are no bars on the head, as with lutinos, you will need to look closely at the eyes. These should not have a white outer circle, which only starts to appear once chicks are about three months old. Once a budgie has gained its adult plumage, it will not be possible to age the bird by looking at it. Many breeders put metal leg bands on their chicks, which carry the year of hatching, such as "14" to indicate 2014.

Many breeders put bands on each bird's leg, with the year the budgie hatched plus a unique identity number.

Cock or hen?

It is much harder to tell the sexes apart when they have just left the nest, but it is possible. Cock birds have ceres that are a slightly darker mauvish shade than those of hens. Look closely, especially just around the nostrils, because this area of the cere is usually paler in young hens. It is usually recommended that you choose a cock budgie as a pet, although hens can talk just as well. Females can be more destructive, pulling at wallpaper, for example, especially when they are older and want to build a nest.

Make sure the travel box has air holes, so the budgie can breathe.

When they are young, a hen (left) and cock (right) are harder to tell apart.

The journey home

Never be tempted to take your new pet home in its cage, because it will become frightened in these surroundings. Instead, budgies travel best in a special box, which is dark, like their nesting box. Check that the box is properly closed, so there is no risk of your pet escaping before you get home. Be careful not to place the box in direct sunlight, because your bird could easily get too hot and die from heatstroke.

Your budgie's home

There are many different types of cage that you could choose as housing for a budgie, but you should always pick a cage that will give your pet plenty of space. It will want to fly from side to side, not up and down. Never be tempted to buy a circular cage, as these are usually too cramped. Instead, choose a large rectangular design, which has perches at either end. The bars on the sides of the cage should not all be upright, but should run horizontally so that the budgie can climb around.

Perches

Most modern cages have plastic perches. You should remove these from the cage and replace them with fresh branches cut from trees. Branches are more comfortable and will also allow your budgie to nibble at the bark with its beak. Check that the tree has not been sprayed with chemicals recently and wash the branches. Position perches so that the budgie's tail feathers will not rub at the ends of the cage, and at a height that allows your pet to sit on them comfortably, without having to stoop.

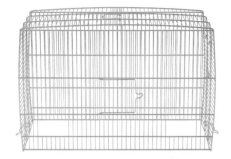

It is important that it is easy to clean your cage. A clean cage will keep your budgie healthy.

Things to remember

A good cage will be expensive, but it will last for the life of your budgie. It helps if the wire unit of the cage is covered with a white or black coating, which prevents the metal from rusting. Some cages come with a detachable plastic base. This makes the cage very easy to clean, but you must always take great care to ensure that your pet cannot escape while the cage is open. The floor of the cage can be lined with special sandsheets, which are easy to change when you clean the cage.

Remove plastic perches from the cage and replace them with wooden ones.

Toys

A wide range of toys are available for budgies, but avoid cluttering your pet's home with too many of these. It is also not a good idea to provide a climbing ladder for a young budgie until it is about six months old, as sometimes the bird may try to climb through the rungs and can become stuck as a result.

Budgies enjoy looking in mirrors. They think their reflection is another bird.

Bird baths let your budgie play in shallow water. This keeps it clean and healthy.

Bath time

A bird bath will keep your budgie's feathers looking shiny. Bird baths attach over the door of the cage. Not all budgies will use a bath like this. If they don't, you should spray them gently using the mist from a clean plant sprayer. You must remove the bird's food first so it does not become damp and then go rotten.

Spray your pet birds regularly with water to help them wash their feathers.

Placing the cage

If you have a tall piece of furniture, then you may be able to put the cage there, with a cloth of some kind to protect the wall, and a mat beneath. If not, you will need to buy a secure stand for the cage, which will keep the cage well off the ground. Always choose a quiet spot in the room, and never position the cage where your bird might get too hot.

Feeding

Budgies feed mainly on grass seeds in the wild, and it is very easy to buy similar seeds for them in packets from pet stores and even supermarkets. There are usually two types of seed in budgie mixes. Millets may come in different shades, ranging from pale yellow through to red, and are round in shape. The other seed, which is known as canary seed, is light brown and oval, with pointed ends.

Budgies crack through the seed husks and eat the softer seed inside. They simply drop the husks.

Food and water containers

Most cages come with seed containers. You can simply brush off the seed husks left behind by the budgie each day, and top up the seeds as required. Budgies must also be given fresh, clean water every day, so you will also need a tubular drinker that attaches to the outside of the cage.

This cage has two seed containers attached to the outside of the cage and a drinker attached to the bars.

Grit and cuttlefish

Budgies use their sharp upper bill to nibble off the seed husk. They do not have teeth, and this is why they eat grit. It passes down into the bird's stomach, along with the seed and other food, and helps to grind up the seed so it can be digested properly. The soft side of a cuttlefish bone helps budgies to keep their bills healthy. It also contains calcium, which is important for healthy bones and eggshells. Hens eat more cuttlefish when they are about to lay their eggs.

Grit can be provided in a container, while there are special clips to hold a cuttlefish bone in place.

Budgies love to nibble at sprays of millet. Place these within easy reach of a perch, holding the stalk in place on the side of the cage with a peg.

Fresh foods and tonics

In addition to seeds, budgies will eat plants such as spinach or dandelion leaves and also slices of apple or carrot. These must be washed first. Dispose of any uneaten fresh food within a day, before it starts to turn rotten.

You can also sprinkle a tonic over these foods, as the powder will stick well to their damp surfaces. A tonic will be especially valuable when your pet is shedding its feathers, helping the new feathers to grow well.

An iodine nibble will help your pet to stay healthy, and hooks directly on to the side of the cage.

Soaked seeds

Soaking the seeds makes them softer to eat, and also makes them more nutritious. Give soaked seeds to your budgie in a separate container from dry ones. Throw away any left uneaten at the end of the day.

1 Put a small amount of seeds in a strainer and rinse them with water. Pour the washed seeds into a bowl.

2 Ask an adult to cover the seeds with hot water. Leave them overnight, and then wash them again.

Taming and talking

You should always give your new pet a day or two to settle down at home with you, before starting to tame it. Most young budgies are naturally not afraid of people, particularly if they were regularly handled in the nest. The easiest way to start is to persuade your budgie to perch on your finger. Always move slowly and carefully, so as not to upset the bird.

Finger-taming

Put your hand in the cage, with your first finger held out and your other fingers curled back into the palm. Slowly bring this finger up to the perch where the budgie is resting, and try to encourage the bird to step on to your finger instead. Place your finger almost under its toes at the front of the perch, and move it slowly over the top of the perch itself. Do this regularly, and before long, you will find that your budgie hops readily on to your finger. You can encourage it by offering a bit of food, such as a small piece of carrot, with the fingers of your other hand.

If you let your budgie out of its cage, place some perches around the room for it to rest on.

1 After your bird has settled into its new cage, let it get to know you by gently stroking it and talking softly.

2 Place your finger in front of the perch. Slowly move it until it is almost touching the budgie's toes. Soon the bird will hop on to it.

Talking

Stick with short lessons, lasting about five minutes. Do not choose long sentences. One of the most important things to teach a pet budgie is your telephone number or address, so that if it does escape, anyone who finds it will be able to contact you. Always speak clearly and slowly, repeating the words until your bird has mastered them, and then you can teach it new ones.

Repeat the words you want your budgie to say many times. Choose short and simple phrases that will be easy for the bird to copy.

Catching and handling

If your budgie will not return to its cage at first, do not chase it around the room, as this will be very stressful for the bird. Turn the lights out, creep up on the budgie, and gently place your fingers around it. Take care, because budgies can sometimes give a painful nip. The best way to hold the bird is to place your fingers on each side of its neck, keeping the wings folded in your hand, so that it will not be able to struggle. It is very important not to press hard on the throat, because you could stop your pet from breathing.

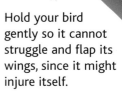

Hold your bird gently so it cannot struggle and flap its wings, since it might injure itself.

Out of the cage

Try to let your budgie out every day to fly around the room. This exercise will keep your bird fit. Never do this without an adult there, as there are likely to be a number of dangers in the room. Make sure the doors and windows are closed, then draw the curtains so the bird does not fly into the glass, and keep cats and dogs out of the room.

Cleaning the cage

You will need to clean out your budgie's cage regularly, because if it is dirty, then your pet could easily become ill. Most people like to line the floor of the cage with sandsheets, which you can buy from a pet store. Always be sure to buy the right size for your cage. When cleaning the cage, you simply need to slide out the floor tray of the cage and drop the old sandsheet carefully into a refuse sack. Then put the new sandsheet in its place on the tray, and push this back into the cage.

Drinkers and food pots

Each week, you will need to wash out your budgie's drinker. If you are using an open container that slides into the cage, then you should clean this thoroughly with soapy water and a paper towel. You may need a special cleaning brush for bottle-type drinkers. You should wear a pair of gloves for this task, and always wash your hands afterwards.

1 Pour a very small amount of dishwashing liquid into the drinker and rinse it well.

2 Wipe out the drinker with a paper towel, taking great care to check the corners are clean.

It is easier to clean the cage if you line the base with a sandsheet. When it is cleaning time, simply throw away the used sheet.

Cleaning the cage

Every six months or so, you may want to wash out your budgie's entire cage, carefully taking it apart for this purpose. You may be able to let your pet fly around the room while you do this, if it is accustomed to coming out of its quarters. This is a good time to replace all the perches too, with some fresh ones that have not been nibbled by the bird.

Budgies outdoors

When they live outside in groups, budgies are housed in buildings called aviaries. These are often built in the shape of a rectangle, but there are circular ones and square ones, too. Aviaries are made of two parts. The snug shelter is similar to a house, where the birds have their food and can sleep at night. This is attached to the outdoor flight, which is made of a wooden framework covered in wire mesh. A safety porch around the door stops budgies escaping as you go in and out.

Aviaries have an enclosed area that is large enough for several birds to fly around. The area is called the flight.

Breeding

If you are keeping male and female budgies together, they will have babies in the spring. You will need to provide them with special nesting boxes to lay their eggs in. These boxes must all be mounted at the same height, to reduce the risk of any squabbling. Hens will lay a clutch of about five white eggs, and these should start to hatch about 18 days later. The breeding pairs will then need special soft food that they can feed to their chicks.

Nesting boxes have a hole for the budgies to go in and come out, and a sliding door so they can be cleaned out easily.

Building an aviary

There are companies that make aviaries, and you can either buy a complete structure or make up your own design using special panels. The aviary should be mounted on a secure base, to prevent it from blowing over in the wind, and the floor must be easy to clean. The roof of the shelter should be covered in thick felt, to keep the inside completely dry, while the area of the flight next to the shelter will need plastic sheeting on the roof and the sides. This will allow the birds to stay outside even if it is raining, without getting wet. Budgies are quite tough birds though, and will not normally need any heating in their aviary during the cold winter.

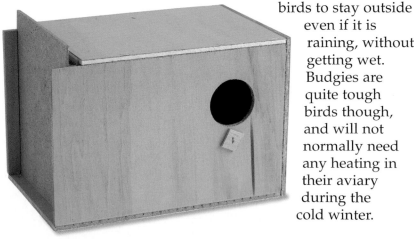

Going away

It is usually not possible to take your budgie with you on vacation, unless you are just going a short distance and will be staying in one place. Many hotels will not allow pets in their rooms. However, it should be quite easy to find a relative or friend prepared to look after your budgie when you are away, especially if you can make the arrangements well in advance.

Preparing to go

You will need to catch your budgie, and transfer it to a carrying box for the journey to its temporary home. Clean the cage thoroughly, as well as the water and food containers, but do not fill these before setting off. Once you arrive, set up the cage and put your budgie back inside. Be sure to take enough seeds and other food to last until you come back.

Do not transport your budgie in its cage. Put it in a ventilated travel box for the journey.

Explain what is needed

You should write out a list of instructions, covering what your budgie needs every day, along with the name, address and phone number of your vet, just in case your pet becomes ill. It will be safer if your budgie is kept permanently in its cage while you are away, because in strange surroundings an accident could easily happen.

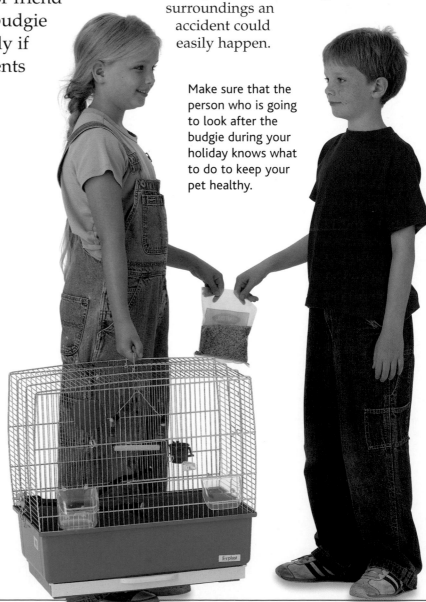

Make sure that the person who is going to look after the budgie during your holiday knows what to do to keep your pet healthy.

Fit and healthy

As long as your budgie's cage is clean, it is unlikely to fall ill. Budgies are most at risk from stomach upsets, and one of the early signs is a change in the appearance of their droppings, which become greenish and soft. A sick budgie may sit with its feathers fluffed up and have no interest in its food. If you suspect that your pet could be ill, take it to a vet as soon as possible. Sometimes budgies will vomit. This can be a sign of illness, although cock birds will sometimes do this to feed their reflections in a mirror. Removing the mirror from the cage for a week or two should solve this problem, but don't delay in speaking to your vet.

Feather problems

Budgies usually drop their feathers each year, and these are replaced by new ones. This process is quite normal and nothing to worry about. Watch out that your budgie does not start to develop bald patches, as it may be pulling its own feathers out. This can have various causes, but using a special bird spray to kill any mites in the cage or on your pet may help to solve the problem.

Budgies sometimes have mites on their feathers. A spray will keep them away.

Checking the beak and claws

As budgies become older, their claws may become overgrown, curling round at their tips. This will make it difficult for your bird to climb on the walls of the cage. Ask your vet to clip the claws. Do the same if the bill starts to become overgrown, although this is less common.

Budgies nibble things to wear down their bills, but older birds might have beaks that are too long.

Tumours

Sometimes, older budgies develop lumps on their bodies, often on their chests. These are likely to be fatty tumours, and they can be removed successfully by an operation, especially while the lumps are still small.

This edition is published by Armadillo,
an imprint of Anness Publishing Ltd, 108 Great Russell Street,
London WC1B 3NA; info@anness.com

www.annesspublishing.com

If you like the images in this book and would like to investigate using
them for publishing, promotions or advertising, please visit our website
www.practicalpictures.com for more information.

Publisher: Joanna Lorenz
Editor: Laura Seber
Designer: Linda Penny
Photographers: Dennis Avon (pp2bl, 4bl, 5–7) and Paul Bricknell
Production Controller: Pirong Wang

The publishers would like to thank Rosie Anness, Alexander Lue,
Alice Mason, and Catherine and Patrick McGovern for appearing
in this book. With special thanks to Ghalib and Janice Al-Nasser for
providing the birds. Picture credit: pp4tr, 17tr and 19tr David Alderton.

PUBLISHER'S NOTE
Although the advice and information in this book are believed to be
accurate and true at the time of going to press, neither the authors nor
the publisher can accept any legal responsibility or liability for any errors
or omissions that may have been made nor for any inaccuracies nor for
any loss, harm or injury that comes about from following instructions
or advice in this book. If you are worried about your pet's health, consult
a veterinarian without delay.

Manufacturer: Anness Publishing Ltd, 108 Great Russell Street,
London WC1B 3NA, England
For Product Tracking go to: www.annesspublishing.com/tracking
Batch: 3149-22808-1127